Lafayette College has a right to be included in the select group of the best institutions in America. Her ideal is to be in the best company scholastically, socially, and athletically and not only to be in the best company but to hold a place of leadership there.

President William Mather Lewis, 1928

LAFAYETTE
MDCCLVII·MDCCCXXXIV

LAFAYETTE
COLLEGE
THEN AND NOW

PHOTOGRAPHED BY TODD BUCHANAN

HARMONY HOUSE
PUBLISHERS-LOUISVILLE

Executive Editors: William Butler and William Strode
Library of Congress Catalog Number: 92-70034
Hardcover International Standard Book Number 1-56469-006-7
Printed in Canada by Friesen Printers, Manitoba, through
Four Colour Imports, Louisville
First Edition printed Spring, 1993 by Harmony House Publishers,
P.O. Box 90, Prospect, Kentucky 40059 (502) 228-2010 / 228-4446
Copyright © 1993 by Harmony House Publishers
Photographs copyright © 1993 by Todd Buchanan

Kirby Library

Introduction

I read, I study, I examine, I listen,
I reflect, and out of all this I try
to form an idea into which
I put as much common sense as I can.

The twenty-year-old Marquis de Lafayette wrote this to his father-in-law in 1777. It appears on the base of the Daniel Chester French statue of the Marquis that stands in front of the chapel at the college that bears his name. The founders of the college chose his name in 1824 " . . . as a testimony of respect for the talents, virtues and signal services of General La Fayette in the great cause of Freedom . . . " The trustees commissioned the statue and chose the inscription it carries to inspire and remind the college's students of the ideals for which the citizen-soldier stood. If the young Marquis were to appear today on the campus, how much sense could he make of what he saw, read, examined or heard about the college bearing his name?

Lafayette College has, during more than a century and a half, demonstrated a continuous search for identity rather than an unswerving march toward fulfillment of the dreams of its founders. The structures added from time to time reflect not only updating and expansion, but shifting from one goal or institutional personality to another. Architecturally, the campus presents a profusion of styles and period pieces consistent with the varying perceptions of the mission of the college. Yet behind all developments and apparent changes of course there stands, as a stabilizing force, the ideal represented by the young Marquis.

Lafayette College was born of a pair of contradictions and conflicts of purpose. The founders, invoking the inspiration of the Marquis, prescribed in the college's charter the teaching of military science, tactics and engineering, in addition to the classical subjects. The first candidate willing to assume the payless presidency objected to military science. The trustees reluctantly let him have his way and had the charter amended. Engineering and science had to wait until the Civil War to be introduced into the curriculum, military science until after World War I.

Pardee Hall, a massive building in Second Empire style, emphasized the essential role of science and engineering in the post-Civil War life of the college. The other early instructional facilities reflect the importance given to technical education — Jenks Hall of Chemistry, later Gayley Hall of Chemistry, the mechanical engineering building and Markle Hall of Mining Engineering.

The science and engineering curricula these structures were meant to house have long since been supplanted by more refined methods of research and specialized courses of study. Pardee therefore, since 1965, houses the liberal arts, and Markle Hall, the administration. Gayley Hall was torn down. Jenks was converted first to biology, then to fine arts and later incorporated into the William E. Simon Center for Economics and Business Administration. Alumni Hall of Engineering and its extension, Dana Hall, together with the remodelled mechanical engineering building house all of the engineering departments. Olin Hall holds physics and chemistry; Kunkel Hall biology; and the old library, Van Wickle, houses geology.

General Lafayette embodied the ideal of the citizen-soldier. Though the college early failed to

Van Wickle Hall

provide military training, large numbers of Lafayette men served in the Civil War and in the nation's foreign wars, and several graduates reached high positions in the military establishment. The ROTC program installed after World War I was a belated response to the wishes of the founders. Initially, ROTC was inadequately housed in the Star Barn, an antiquated astronomical observatory located where Markle Hall now stands. Then the military training program came of age and, in 1930, moved into specially-designed quarters in the basement of the ornate new Kirby Hall of Civil Rights. In the early 1960s, the program received its own off-campus building, Fretz House, remaining there until the government closed the program in 1991 in a budget-trimming initiative. Both the founders and the young Marquis would have regretted this development. It was appropriate that the history department then moved into Fretz House.

The founders did not want the college "priest ridden," and Article 8 of the charter specifically charges that no one shall be deprived of rights and privileges at the college because of his religion. The young Marquis would have approved. The first president, however, was a Presbyterian minister. By 1849 the college came under the direction of the Presbyterian Synod of Philadelphia. In 1851 Professor Lyman Coleman joined the faculty and made the Bible the foundation of all studies. For over a century the overwhelming majority of students and all of the faculty were protestant. Colton Memorial Chapel, a handsome building designed in 1916 by the foremost architects of the time, Carrere and Hastings, reflects the college's historical affiliation with the Presbyterian Church. Today there are no required religion courses or mandatory chapel services.

Brainerd Hall, now called Hogg Hall after its donor, J. Renwick Hogg, Class of 1878, was built to house the Brainerd Society, an evangelical and social service organization to which almost all students belonged. Changing its name in 1944 was not inappropriate since the original purpose of the society had disappeared and most of its social service functions had been taken over by the administration. The building became an inadequate student center. While it still houses the chaplain's office and an interfaith chapel, the second floor has been renovated as the Career Planning and Placement Center.

Until World War II the college was a small, close-knit community. Most students belonged to fraternities that had built their own houses on campus following their own architectural instincts. A few residence halls — "Dorm Row," South College and Easton Hall — housed the freshmen and independents. The senior faculty lived in houses on campus and the junior faculty, mainly young, single men with short-term contracts, lived as proctors in the dormitories.

After World War II, the college's enrollment mushroomed and campus space became scarce. Lifestyles changed. The faculty—preferring some private life—moved off campus. As the number of students increased, fraternities no longer satisfied all the housing and social needs of a more and more diverse group of undergraduates. "Social dormitories" of red brick appeared. More residence halls of the same building material sprouted up. Marquis Hall was built in 1960 to provide a student social center and dining facilities, and McKelvy House, several blocks from the main campus, was opened as a college scholars residence.

When in 1970 women were admitted to degree programs, the number of students was fixed at 2,000. But the problems of residence, dining, and social life were exacerbated. The Farinon College Center, completed in 1991, more than meets many of these needs. As student expectations continue to expand, new needs will be identified.

When a good portion of the library was ruined in the fire that almost destroyed Pardee Hall in 1897, it became all too apparent that the college's library facilities had long been inadequate. The Van Wickle Memorial Library was the answer. This building grew along with the collection it housed until it again became evident that something larger and grander was called for. The David B. Skillman Library, built in 1963, was designed to serve 1,500 students. A northern wing added in 1987 provided very necessary study and computer facilities.

There was a time when the half-moon area called the Quadrangle was the private domain of the campus cow. She yielded to athletics—first baseball, then football—in the decades after the Civil War. As sports became more and more a factor in the lives of the students, a gymnasium was built in 1884 (where Kirby Hall now stands). By 1894 the Quadrangle was no longer adequate, and outdoor athletics moved to newly acquired territory — March Field. While this field may have been large enough before chunks of it were claimed, piece by piece, for classrooms, dormitories and fraternity houses, the makeshift stands were not. In the twenties a new structure — Alumni Memorial Gymnasium — was built. Fisher Field provided firmer concrete stands. And as with facilities for every other activity, these in turn proved inadequate. In 1969 Metzgar Fields opened on a tract owned by the College north of the city and in 1973 the Kirby Field House took over most of the activities serviced by Alumni Gym.

Since the first Arbor Day in 1885, when the graduating class initiated a tree-planting tradition, many exotic trees have been added to the campus landscape. In 1909 the Olmstead brothers, designers of Manhattan's Central Park, developed a campus plan which provided a blueprint of order and arboreal harmony. Although portions of the plan were realized,

the grounds suffered from inadequate maintenance during the decades following the Depression. Beginning with the Bergethon administration, more care was given to landscaping. Lawns replaced rice paddies, and trees and shrubs were planted and cared for. Landscape planning became an important part of all new construction. The campus is a riot of colorful trees in bloom in spring. Throughout the summer, perennials and annuals flourish in well-tended flower beds.

The young Marquis was not only a champion of liberty, but as a French aristocrat, a man of culture, too. In a visit to the campus before 1983 he would have been disappointed at the absence of any monument to the fine arts and only slightly appeased to learn that one had been dreamed about for a long time. After 1984 he would have appreciated the presence of the Williams Center for the Arts, quite likely intrigued at the turn architecture had taken.

The campus and its buildings meet the demands of people and of function. The requirements of increasing numbers, changing goals and tastes and, perhaps of greatest importance, changing perceptions of the college's mission mean constant shifting in the scene. The demands have changed since the 1830s when a handful of students and faculty first pursued higher education (supplemented by a program of manual labor) on the south bank of the Lehigh River. In the late twentieth century, 2,000 students, 21,000 alumni, a faculty of 200 and an administrative and service staff of 350 continue to enact the drama on the adaptable stage that is Lafayette College.

Were the young Marquis to return to reflect on the scene he might possibly sense that the institution does honor the motives of the founders in naming their college after our revolutionary hero.

Albert W. Gendebien '34
Emeritus Professor of History

Kirby Hall of Civil Rights

Williams Center for the Arts

A passion for learning has long been evident at Lafayette; our proud and formidable history testifies to it, to a healthy zest for innovation, and to a willingness to find pathways to growth that are consistent with educational integrity.

From the inaugural address of President Robert I. Rotberg, November 3, 1990

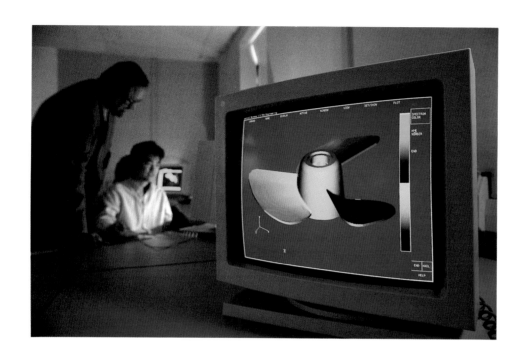

...because of the presence of both strong engineering and liberal arts programs within one undergraduate institution, Lafayette College has the opportunity to pioneer in areas that bridge the role of technology in our society and the traditional liberal arts.

From David W. Ellis's inaugural address, October 20, 1978

Our curriculum as well as campus life must encourage the rich and broad experience necessary to the discovery of self and to the voluntary commitment to a demanding code of values.

From K. Roald Bergethon's inaugural address, October 18, 1958

McKelvy House

The vine now planted here, I trust, will spread over the East and the West, the North and the South, carrying its branches throughout all our borders covering all the country with the beautiful shade and giving to the students of the institution honor, strength, and truth.

William Cullen Bryant, speaking at the post-Commencement luncheon, 1877

*We feel confident that there are few, if any colleges in the
land, where more care is bestowed on the student, and where
they have better literary and moral advantages.*

Faculty Report to the Trustees, 1856

Colton Chapel

The old alumnus will return to see many of the old landmarks which figured in his college career, gone. Men will look in vain for the old Martien steps where, in the twilight, the stirring songs were sung of Alma Mater. The wily Sophomore will miss the McKeen Hall balcony, so convenient for Freshmen who have no time to study hydraulics in the classroom.... Let us pause and sigh.

The Lafayette, 1900

Simon Wing of Skillman Library

Alumni Memorial Gymnasium

Soles Hall

FARMON COLLEGE CENTER

Farinon College Center

Greek Week tricycle race

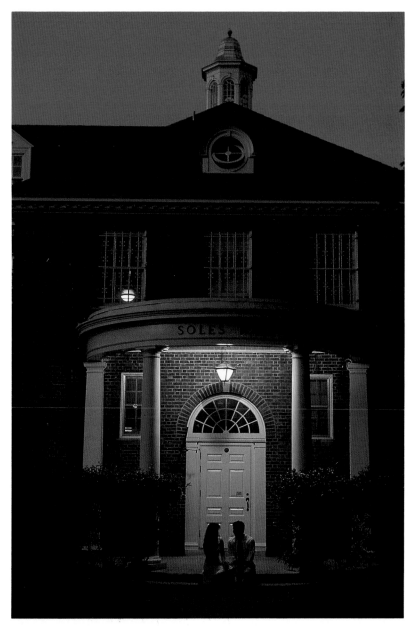

Early morning Crew Club practice on the Lehigh River.

49

Lafayette vs. Yale

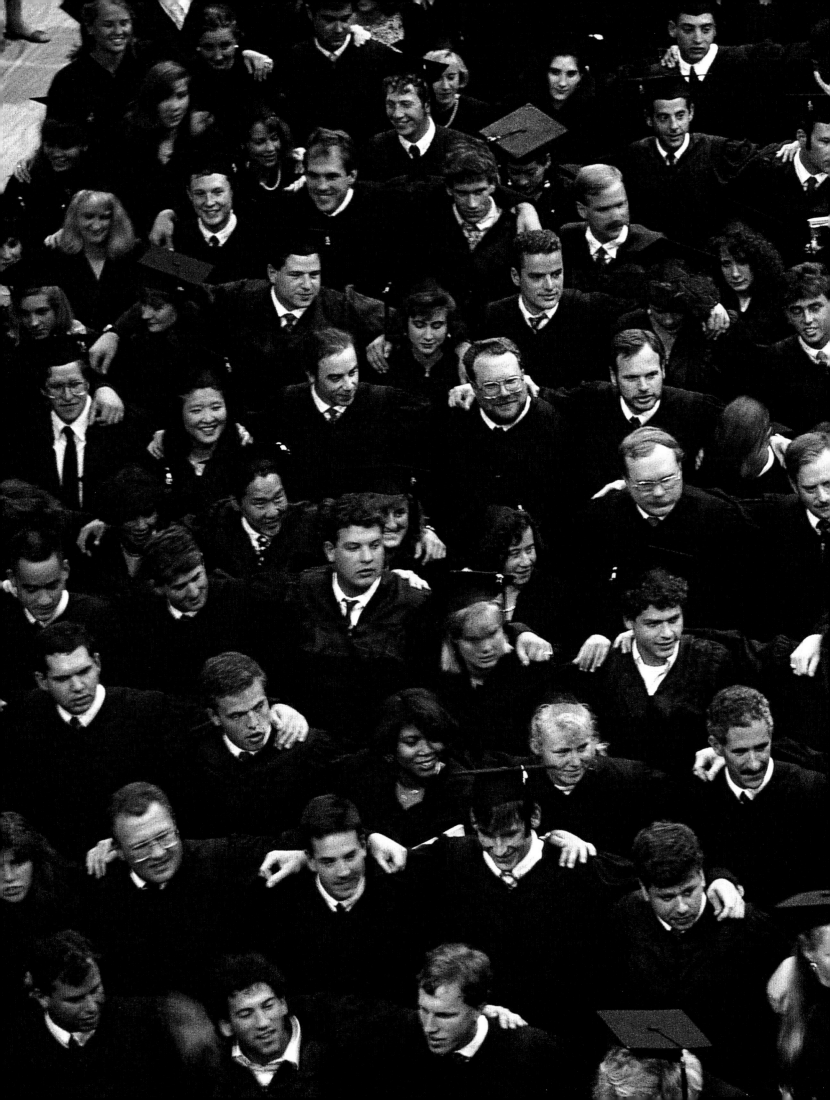

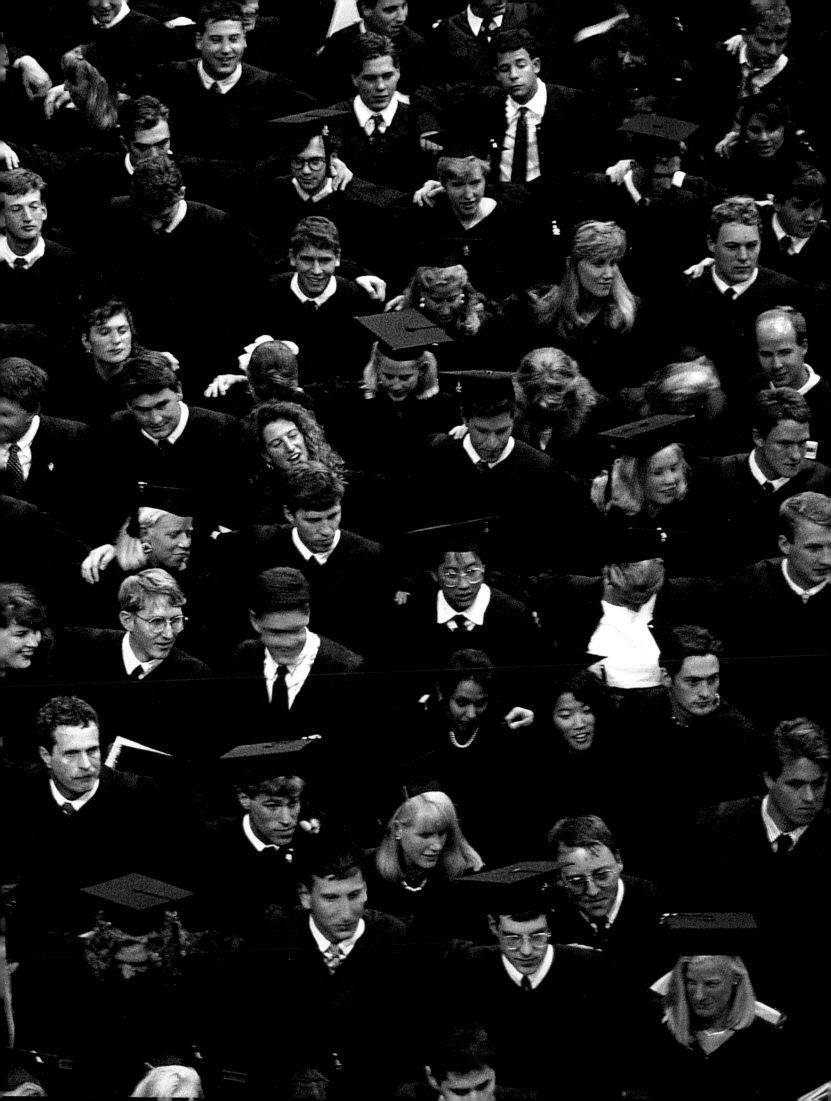

A look back at Lafayette

Early view of South College, the first major college building. The center section, completed in 1834, was designed by President George Junkin and built by Junkin and Lafayette students. The east wing was added in 1869 and the west wing with its clock tower, in 1873.

The college library in the east wing of South College, circa 1880.

The South College clock tower engulfed in flames shortly before its collapse at 11:32 p.m. on March 3, 1956.

View of South College showing the restored west wing with its new, less elaborate clock tower, completed in 1957, and the new center section completed in 1962. With the razing of the center section in 1961, no portion of the original college edifice remained.

Lafayette's grandest building, Pardee Hall, was built to house the college's new scientific school. Completed in 1873, it was designed by John McArthur, Jr., architect of Philadelphia's City Hall. Its quarter-of-a-million-dollar price was paid by Hazelton (Pa.) mining magnate, Ario Pardee.

Electrical engineering laboratory in Pardee Hall, 1907.

Pardee Hall in ruins, 1879. Only seven years after its dedication, Pardee burned to the walls, the result of carelessness in the chemistry lab. In 1897, Pardee burned again. This time it was the result of arson—the fire was set by a former professor of moral philosophy and ethics.

Lafayette's first gymnasium, built in 1884 and demolished in the 1920s. The building was an exact copy of the Vanderbilt University gymnasium, which is still standing.

The Traill Green Astronomical Observatory, erected in 1864 on the site now occupied by Colton Chapel. Known affectionately as the "Star Barn," it was moved to what is currently the site of Markle Hall in 1914. Torn down in 1928, its stones were used to form the gateway to the college at the end of Third Street.

Gayley Hall of Chemistry and Metallurgy. Built in 1922 and torn down in the early 1960s, it stood on the present site of Skillman Library.

Old McKeen Hall, the central building of Dormitory Row. Constructed in 1871, the dormitory was originally called Central House. It was demolished in 1957.

The President's House was built in 1867 as a personal residence by President William C. Cattell. In 1884, John I. Blair bought the house and presented it to the college as a residence for the college president.

View of the original Italian gardens of McKelvey House. Built in 1888, "Oakhurst," as the house was originally called, was designed by the leading American architectural firm McKim, Mead, and White.

Assembly Room in Brainerd (now Hogg) Hall, circa 1907. Lafayette's only Gothic Revival building was built in 1902 as a home for the Brainerd Society and as a social center. Its name was changed to honor its donor, James Renwick Hogg, in 1944.

Van Wickle Library, built in 1899. This view shows the original eyebrow windows in the roof, which are no longer present.

The original reading room in Van Wickle. The Tiffany window depicting Sir Philip Sidney on the Field of Zutphen is in its original location in the western end of the building. It was later moved to the eastern end.

Colton Chapel, built in 1916, was designed by the architectural firm of Carrere and Hastings, noted for bringing the Beaux-Arts style to America and for such buildings as the New York Public Library.

Alumni Memorial Gymnasium, completed in 1924.

Markle Hall, constructed in 1929. Originally the John Markle Hall of Mining Engineering, it became the Markle Administration Building in 1964.

Kirby Hall of Civil Rights. Completed in 1930, it was built by trustee Fred Morgan Kirby to house the department of government and law. The donor provided for the finest building materials available; the lobby shown here is constructed of Italian travertine. The architects were the New York firm of Warren and Wetmore, designers of Grand Central Station.

Phi Delta Theta fraternity house, built 1907.

The Phi Kappa Psi house progressing down Sullivan Lane in 1971. The house was moved from its original site near the north end of Skillman Library to March Field.

Chi Phi fraternity house.

Civil engineering students, circa 1893, with the truss bridge erected every year as a class project between Pardee Hall and Colton Chapel.

Class in mine rescue, 1929.

Electrical engineering laboratory.

Botanical students of the Class of 1874 at "Pot-Rock" near St. Anthony's Nose on the Delaware River above Easton.

Bonfire on the quad, 1904.

The Class of 1906 battles the Class of 1907 in the traditional banner scrap in 1903. The sophomores, armed with paper bags of flour, attempt to gain control of the freshman flag, suspended from a campus building.

The cane rush, another traditional contest between freshmen and sophomores. At the crack of the gun, the two classes charged each other vying to get the most hands on the cane at the end of ten minutes of fierce struggle.

Senior "Peerade," 1915.

Students stage a mock protest of prohibition, circa 1920s.

The Class of 1892's Calculus Play, June 21, 1890, at the Able Opera House in Easton. The play was an outgrowth of the Lafayette tradition of the cremation of calculus, in which students symbolically (and sometimes literally) burned their hated calculus texts.

Peace symbols at Commencement, 1970.

Rally for coeducation, 1968. The sign in the background reads "Coeducation Now."

Student demonstrators protest American involvement in the Vietnam War at the annual ROTC Awards Ceremony, Fisher Field, May 5, 1969.

Susan L. Trotter (left) and Joyce S. Cohen, Class of 1974, the first women to enroll at Lafayette after coeducation was approved.

Sheila Drummond (left) and Darlyne Bailey volunteer with young participants in the "Black Children Can" program, April 1972. This tutorial and motivational program was sponsored by Lafayette's Association of Black Collegians.

Dormitory scene, early 1970s.

Lafayette cheerleader with the leopard, 1970.

Lafayette vs. Lehigh in women's lacrosse, April 1988. Lafayette was victorious, 14-0.

Baseball action, March Field, circa 1916.

The 1881 baseball team.

Waiting to play.

The 1924 baseball team. Legendary coach Bill Coughlin is at top center on left.

Charles R. "Babe" Rinehart, Class of 1898, and friend.

Lafayette's first great football team, 1896. The football season of 1896, marked by an astounding victory over Penn and marred only by a tie with Princeton, catapulted the maroon and white into the first ranks of collegiate gridiron contenders.

Gridiron action on March Field, circa 1917.

The Lafayette-Lehigh game, March Field, 1920. Lafayette won this famous contest for ten straight seasons between 1919 and 1928.

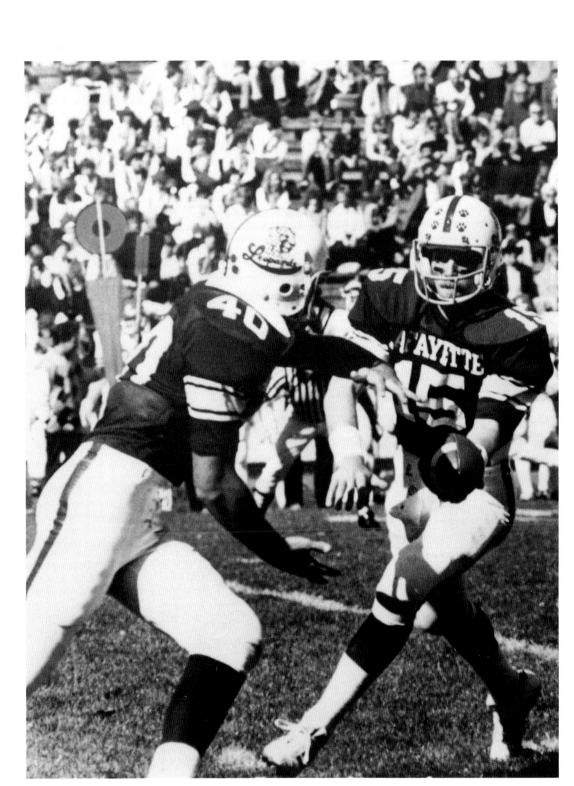

The hand-off, 1981. The 1981 season marked two milestones—Lafayette's 100th year of football and the rookie year for head coach Bill Russo.

The 1915 soccer team.

The track team, circa 1917.

Todd Tripucka, Class of 1976, shoots against St. John's in the first round of the 1975 National Invitation Tournament at Madison Square Garden.

The 1940 ice hockey team.

Wrestling action, circa 1950s.

The 1937 tennis team.

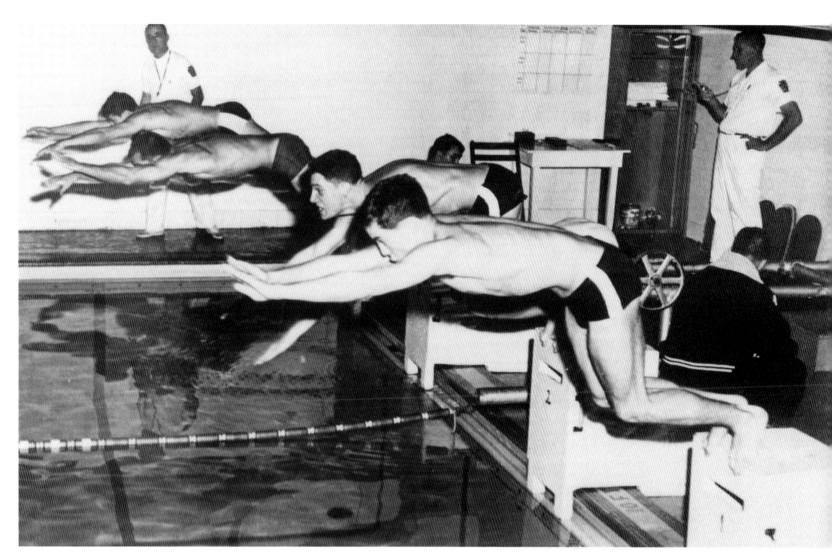

Swimming the 50-yard freestyle.

Tents on March Field during World War I. In 1918, Lafayette became a military camp to prepare men for the war. In addition to vocational and military training, the college continued the academic education of its students through the Student Army Training Corps program.

Scenes from Camp Lafayette, 1918.

Editorial Board of The Touchstone, *Lafayette literary magazine, 1898-99.*

Editorial Board of The Lafayette, *1897-98.*

The annual Shakespearean play performed during Commencement festivities, early 1920s.

The college band, 1924.

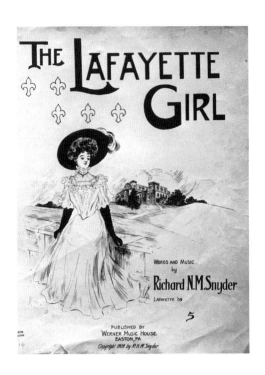

Faculty show, "The Faculty Flame," 1953. Performers were Jim and Tinker Vitelli and Dick Rudden.

Formal dance, World War II era.

Frolicking at the shore.

Dance, early 1970s.

Theta Delta Chi, Interfraternity Weekend, 1953.

Professor Francis Andrew March in his classroom. Appointed professor of English Language and Comparative Philology in 1857, March had the distinction of being the first professor of English at an American college or university. During his long and distinguished career, he received international recognition for his contributions to the study of the English language.

Alumni reunion, 1919.

New York Alumni Association dinner in honor of Francis March, St. Regis Hotel, February 9, 1906.

The Class of 1880's twenty-year reunion, June 1900.